Nick and Nora

The Couple Who Taught America How to Drink

NICK AND NORA

The Couple Who Taught America How to Drink

Quips, Quotes, and Cocktails
by Michael Turback

Index

The Life and Times of Nick and Nora….. 1

Happy Days are Here Again….. 7

The Shaking Rhythm….. 13

The Manhattan Fox-Trot….. 17
    Pierre's Manhattan
    Sherman Cocktail
    All Right Cocktail
    Saratoga Cocktail
    Rob Roy
    Bobby Burns
    Chancellor
    Up-to-Date
    Brown University Cocktail
    Waldorf
    Palmetto
    Scofflaw
    Marconi Wireless
    Algonquin
    Remember the Maine
    Stork Club Manhattan

The Bronx Two-Step….. 35
    Bronx, The
    Boothby's Bronx Cocktail
    Silver Bronx

Income Tax Cocktail
Satan's Whiskers
Queens Cocktail

The Martini Waltz….. 43
Martini Cocktail
Martinez
Abbey Martini
Turf Club
Gin and It
Zaza
Hanky-Panky
Barry Cocktail, The
Colony Cocktail
Cooperstown
Cornell Cocktail
Gibson
Gin Cocktail
The Crisp
McCutcheon, The
Astoria

Heyday of the Cocktail….. 61
Monkey Gland
Maiden's Blush
Champagne Cocktail
Widow's Kiss
Bosom Caresser

Buck's Fizz
Mary Pickford
Ace of Clubs
Aviation
Jack Rose
Clover Club
Southside Cocktail
Chicago Cocktail
Harlem Cocktail
Blue Moon
Horse's Neck
Mamie Taylor
Monkey Wrench
Puritan, The
Vanishing Cream
Glover's Mange Cure
Golden Slipper
Blackthorne Sour
Xanthia
Yellow Parrot
Warday's Cocktail
Fifth Avenue
Don't Give Up the Ship
Napoléon
King Cole
Fanciulli
Savoy Corpse Reviver
IBF Pick-Me-Up

Toronto
Guggenheim Cocktail
Old Hat
Barbary Coast
Dubonnet Cocktail
Turf Club
Princeton Cocktail
Yale Cocktail
Skinner and Eddy
Harry's Cocktail
Alaska Cocktail
Bijou, The
Alberto, The
Atta Boy Cocktail
Rolls-Royce
Tuxedo
Alcazer
Boulevardier
Champs-Élysées

The Life and Times of Nick and Nora

> Nick Charles (carrying a tray of drinks):
> *Here's that man again! Ammunition! Highballs and cocktails – the long and short of it.*

Repeal of Prohibition in the United States was accomplished with the passage of the Twenty-first Amendment to the Constitution on December 5, 1933. While the Noble Experiment may have colored the act of drinking in shades of rebellion, after repeal alcohol was in good standing again. Social drinking became not only respectable but ubiquitous.

Hollywood celebrated the new permissiveness toward imbibing. The most notable example was a series of popular films starring William Powell and Myrna Loy. Metro-Goldwyn-Mayer produced *The Thin Man* with an eye on Repeal, hoping to capture the mood of thirsty Americans.

Powell had already played detective Philo Vance, and had appeared in a few light comedies. Myrna Loy, meanwhile, had played in small roles during the Silent Era before graduating to serious parts. After Powell and Loy appeared together in *Manhattan Melodrama*, director W.S. Van Hyde reunited the pair in *The Thin Man*, a comic detective story based on a Dashiell Hammett novel. Their characters were named Nick and Nora Charles – Nick a hard-drinking, retired private detective, and Nora a wealthy heiress.

They loved their liquor – loved it all the more coming off the traumatic experience of Prohibition, when the public flocked to both the movies and nightclubs. It was a set designer's vision of sophisticated nightspots that became the boozy playground for Nick and Nora and a night on the town – movie audiences were surprised to see people openly drinking on the screen in lush surroundings.

Nick and Nora live life entirely the way they want to – they've created a world of their own that's sophisticated and mischievous and intelligent and funny and full of adventure. And the correct intoxicants. Alcohol is as much a part of the marriage as the couple is, but that isn't a bad thing. The drinks simply function as another act that binds the two together, a lubricant for their quick tongues and witty dialog. It is at once the surface activity and practiced ritual but never seen as an all-consuming vice.

Brian Lokker explains, "For most people, the fact that Nick and Nora's banter was usually lubricated by alcohol did not detract from their appeal – especially to movie audiences who had only been released a few months earlier from fourteen years of Prohibition."

"What is perhaps most striking about Nick and Nora," writes Christopher Orr, "is not their easy blend of comedy and drama or their balanced sexual dynamic, but rather their carefree booziness." In *Love on the Rocks*, author Lori Rotskoff writes, "After fourteen years of Prohibition, *The Thin Man* celebrated the return of licit alcohol with a humorous and exaggerated vengeance. Certain the sheer excess of the couple's drinking spoofed the decadent extremism pursued by a minority of drinkers. But despite its gently satirical tone, the film nonetheless condoned drinking as a sign of worldly sophistication."

In her review, Lauren Ennis asserts, "The only thing that sparkles more than the Charles' wit is their seemingly endless supply of Champagne. Throughout the holiday season in which *The Thin Man* takes place, the couple keeps the harsh realities of Depression-era life at bay with the help of a Prohibition-era invention – the cocktail. There is scarcely a moment, let alone a scene, in which either Nick or Nora are without a drink in their hands or a slight slur in their speech." Stuart Henderson affirms, "The repartée and banter between the two wealthy (and always reluctant) detectives revolves around cutesy marriage jokes and an insatiable thirst for martinis."

In *The Book of Gin*," Richard Barnett observes, "*The*

Thin Man films reminded American drinkers that they were allowed to have a good time again, no matter what clouds might be building up on their horizons."

Audiences adored *The Thin Man*, and so did the critics. The film earned Academy Award nominations for Best Picture, Best Actor, Best Director, and Best Adapted Screenplay. Five sequels followed, with Van Dyke directing three of them, *After the Thin Man* (1936), *Another Thin Man* (1939), and *Shadow of the Thin Man* (1941). The other two were produced after Van Dyke's death in 1943 and included *The Thin Man Goes Home* (1944), directed by Richard Thorpe, and *Song of the Thin Man* (1947), helmed by Edward Buzzell.

According to writer Joseph Lanza, "the cocktail evolved from a universal symbol of licentiousness into one of class and civility." *The Thin Man* films are permeated with drinking scenes in which Nick and Nora not only glamorize drinking, they depict intoxicants as an enhancement rather than a detriment to marital relations. They taught the men and women of post-Prohibition America how to drink.

This volume celebrates the life and times of Nick and Nora and the touchstones of civilized cocktail culture with drink recipes that endured and survived Mr. Volstead. In the words of Nick Charles: "Now my friends, if I may propose a little toast. Let us eat, drink and be merry, for tomorrow we die.

Happy Days Are Here Again

Reporter: Why are you in town?
Nick: My wife is on a bender. I'm trying to sober her up.

It's no surprise that Nick and Nora Charles captivated audiences when the sleuthing couple tipsily arrived on the big screen in 1934. Prohibition in America had just recently been repealed. The nation was in the mood for a drink, and Nick and Nora happily imbibed. In Dashiell Hammett's novel, Nick downs 33 drinks (about one every six pages), while in the film he slows down to a mere 21 drinks (about one every four minutes). In *Booze and the Private Eye*, author Rita Elizabeth Rippetoe suggests it is possible to view *The Thin Man* "as practically a non-stop drinking binge."

In a 2002 reflection on the film, Roger Ebert described *The Thin Man* series as pure entertainment, where "The drinks are the lubricant for dialogue of elegant wit and wicked timing, used by a character who is decadent on the surface but fundamentally brave and brilliant."

"In the world of *The Thin Man*," further explains Richard Barnett in *The Book of Gin*, "the Great Experiment is elided, and Martinis, along with dancing, laughter, parties and fine clothes, are not objects of guilt or shame but simply part of daily life. In this sense, *The Thin Man* films remind American drinkers that they were allowed to have a good time again."

Historian W. J. Rorabaugh contemplated drinking in *The Thin Man* films: "Amid the Great Depression, it was perfectly acceptable to drown one's cares in alcohol. The proof that one was having a good time was shown by slurred speech, by falling down, by wild dancing, by loud talking and laughing, and by singing off-key. Americans, perhaps, yearned to throw off Victorian propriety as well as the restrictive burdens of Prohibition. Nick and Nora were showing them how to do it."

In *Thoughts on The Thin Man*, Danny Reid observes, "Embodied by the sleepy-eyed Willian Powell with a mildly detectable slur and a slight wobble in his step, there are few moments when Nick does not seem to be half in the bag, whether he's decked out in a tuxedo hosting a dinner party or taking BB gun potshots at the Christmas tree in his pajamas."

In the world of Nick and Nora, alcohol is frequently shown to be a good way to cope with trouble. Perhaps this was an effective sales pitch in the early post-Prohibition era, when Americans, especially those of a new generation that had never before tasted legal alcohol, have to be coaxed into drinking. Millions of Americans lived vicariously through the lives of Nick and Nora.

In a *Time* magazine analysis of *The Thin Man*, Gary Susman writes, "Nick and Nora remain the prime examples of what we think we're like when we drink: sexier and smarter."

According to Charles McGrath of *The New Yorker*, "People in the thirties thought drunkenness was much funnier than we do now, and in *The Thin Man*, at least, you can see why. 'Tight' is the word Nick and Nora use to describe their usual condition, but in fact drink makes them the opposite. He has a wonderful rubbery walk, and a way of ever so slightly slurring his words (which must have been much harder to pull off than full-on drunk-acting). And the great joke, or trick, of the movie is that drink does nothing to dull their thought processes – either their wisecracking or his crime-solving. It only makes them smarter."

Kim Morgan points out that "Nick Charles likes to drink. Nick Charles likes to drink a lot – copious amounts of alcohol – one glass emptied in one hand, the other reaching for another with an elegance and panache that's as graceful as a tipsy, never fully drunk dancer. She, as in Nora Charles, drinks too, with merriment and style and with routine like Nick, and she also consumes liberally, almost as much or as much as her husband."

"Powell plays the character with a lyrical alcoholic slur that waxes and wanes but never topples either way into inebriation or sobriety," insists Bill Damon. "The drinks are the lubricant for dialogue of elegant wit and wicked timing, used by a character who is decadent on the surface but fundamentally brave and brilliant."

Writing in *The Atlantic*, Christopher Orr observes, "As Nick and Nora, Powell and Loy subverted the classic detective film with comic aplomb and presented an impressively modern vision of marriage as an association of equals. They were also cinema's most glamorous dipsomaniacs, a reminder of a bygone era when Hollywood could still imagine that charm, taste, and good humor might go hand-in-hand with the copious consumption of distilled spirits."

Caroline Jean Acker notes, "*The Thin Man* portrays the bar as a place where chic urbanites deploy wit and display tony wardrobes. Nora's downing of five martinis in rapid succession and Nick's kidding response to her hangover the next day helped create an acceptance of heavy levels of social drinking."

"About the nonstop alcohol consumption in *The Thin Man*, and its potentially dire influence on public morality,"

Emily W. Leider reports, "a concerned woman, possibly a theater manager, wrote to the Production Code Administration's Joseph Breen to observe, 'It seems to me what has been taken out in vulgarity has been put back in drinking.'"

"Not since Nick and Nora Charles virtually made the dry martini into the national drink," writes Vincent Canby, "has there been quite so much boozing in a movie without hidden consequences."

"Arguably *The Thin Man* glamorized fashionable drinking more than any other movie," declares Garrett Peck in *The Prohibition Hangover*, "until HBO produced its *Sex and the City* TV series in the late 1990s."

> *Nick: If the party gets rough, duck.*
> *Nora: I'm practically under the table now, but not the way I like to be.*

THE SHAKING RHYTHM

Nick: *"The important thing is the rhythm. Always have rhythm in your shaking. Now a Manhattan you shake to fox-trot time, a Bronx to two-step time, a Dry Martini you always shake to waltz time."*

New York's Knickerbocker Bar is remembered for its role in the dawn of the modern Martini, mixed behind the grand mahogany counter by Italian immigrant bartender Martini di Arma di Taggia. Mr. Martini played an important role in the evolution of the venerable cocktail when he first married London Dry Gin and Noilly Prat Dry Vermouth, added a dash of orange bitters, then christened the resulting concoction after himself.

While bar practice now favors a non-controversial stirring of the Martini, during the 1930s, Marco Hattem, the Turkish bartender of New York's Colony restaurant popularized the shake. In *The Colony*, Iles Brody's book about the legendary restaurant, he explains that "Marco shakes his Martinis merrily, and pours them into their appropriate glasses where they glitter like crystal." In *The Stork Club Bar Book,* author Lucius Beebe takes the club's preparation of the Martini one step further: "Management will oblige by having them compounded in a cement mixer or butter churn if that is what the customer wants."

Shaking introduces air bubbles into the mix, resulting in a cloudy appearance and a somewhat different texture on the tongue when compared with a stirred drink. Most connoisseurs believe that shaking a Martini is a faux pas, supposedly because the shaking "bruises" the gin (a term referring to a slight bitter taste that can allegedly occur when gin is shaken).

If ever a couple possessed complementary drinking rhythms, it would have to be Nick and Nora Charles, the glamorous cocktail-swilling duo of Dashiell Hammett's *The Thin Man*.

> *Reporter: Well, can't you tell us anything about the case?*
> *Nick: Yes, it's putting me way behind in my drinking.*

THE MANHATTAN FOX-TROT

Nora: Is that my drink over there?
Nick : What were you drinking?
Nora : Rye.
Nick (finishing her drink in one gulp): Yes, that's yours.

It's a sophisticated drink that embraces the energy of the place after which it's named. The Manhattan has a much-debated history, but everyone agrees the drink was indeed conceived in New York City in the second half of the nineteenth century. Attractive enough on their own, its ingredients become positively alluring when mixed, which explains the passion of devotees. While it's classically made with whiskey, sweet vermouth and bitters, like its namesake, the Manhattan has always been adaptable. "Make no mistake about it," writes Lucius Beebe in *The Stork Club Bar Book,* the Manhattan was the archetypal short mixed drink and blazed a trail for all others to follow."

Nora: Are you packing?
Nick: Yes dear, I'm putting away this liquor.

Pierre's Manhattan

While the drink may have been created for Lady Randolph Churchill, Winston Churchill's mother, at the Manhattan Club in the 1870s, it was at Pierre's, on Forty-fifth Street immediately west of Fifth Avenue, where the Manhattan Cocktail was introduced to New York society. "Some connoisseurs or poseurs contend that in mixing a Manhattan cocktail, the whiskey must always be put into the mixing glass before the vermouth," writes Charles Brown in *The Gun Club Drink Book*, "but just why, deponent sayeth not."

> **2 ounces rye whiskey**
> **1 ounce Italian vermouth**
> **1 dash Angostura bitters**
> **Maraschino cherry with stem**

Combine ingredients in a mixing glass filled with cracked ice. Stir briskly and strain into a cocktail glass. Garnish with cherry.

Sherman Cocktail

The legendary Waldorf-Astoria bar was a favorite haunt of many of the financial elite of the New York City, including Diamond Jim Brady, Buffalo Bill Cody and Bat Masterson. A number of cocktails were invented at the bar, including the Rob Roy, the Bobbie Burns, and the Sherman Cocktail. Essentially a twist on the Manhattan with the addition of absinthe and the partnership of bitters, the drink was immortalized in Albert Steven Crockett's *Old Waldorf-Astoria Bar Book*.

> 2 ounces rye whiskey
> 1 ounce Italian vermouth
> 1/2 barspoon absinthe
> 1 dash Angostura bitters
> 1 dash orange bitters
> lemon peel

Combine liquid ingredients in a mixing glass filled with cracked ice. Stir briskly and strain into a cocktail glass. Express lemon peel over the glass, rub around the rim, and drop in.

All Right Cocktail

Tom Bullock was the longtime bartender at the St. Louis Country Club and the first African-American bartender to publish a cocktail manual. That 1917 book, *The Ideal Bartender*, includes Mr. Bullock's All Right Cocktail, his concoction of three elemental ingredients that gave a nod to the Manhattan while fashioning itself into something genuine and original. A mere dash of bitters adds a touch of complexity to this perfectly rounded cocktail.

> 1 1/2 ounces rye whiskey
> 3/4 ounce orange curacao
> 1 dash Angostura bitters

Combine ingredients in a mixing glass filled with cracked ice. Shake vigorously and strain into a coupe glass.

Saratoga Cocktail

In 1867, John H. Morrisey built the Club House Casino in Saratoga, New York, a gathering place for gamblers and card players like "Diamond Jim" Brady (and companion Lillian Russell), "Bet a Million" Gates, and bookie "Irish John" Cavanaugh. *New York World* reporter Nellie Bly once branded Saratoga "Our Wickedest Summer Resort." Popularized among the sporting crowd, the Saratoga Cocktail first appears in print in Jerry Thomas' 1887 *Bar-Tender's Guide*. (Although he calls for shaking with ice, the drink benefits from being stirred instead to preserve clarity.

> 1 ounce rye whiskey
> 1 ounce Cognac
> 1 ounce Italian vermouth
> 2 dashes Angostura bitters
> lemon peel

Combine ingredients in a mixing glass filled with cracked ice. Stir briskly and strain into a cocktail glass. Express lemon peel over the glass, rub around the rim, and drop in.

Rob Roy

Invented in 1894 by a bartender at the Old Waldorf Men's Bar, the drink was named in honor of the premiere of *Rob Roy*, an operetta based upon Scottish folk hero Robert Roy MacGregor. Like the original Manhattan, a Scotch-based Rob Roy can be made with sweet, dry, or tempered with both sweet and dry vermouth, in which case the drink is called an "Affinity." Replace vermouth with Benedictine in a Rob Roy and you have yourself a "Bobby Burns." Contrast equal parts Scotch and sweet vermouth with blood orange juice and Cherry Heering, and you have yourself a Blood & Sand (named for the 1922 Rudolph Valentino film).

> 2 ounces Scotch whiskey
> 1 ounce Italian vermouth
> 1 dash Angostura bitters
> Maraschino cherry with stem

Combine ingredients in a mixing glass filled with cracked ice. Stir briskly and strain into a cocktail glass. Garnish with cherry.

Bobby Burns

A slight modification to the Rob Roy makes all the difference to a drink named after Robert Burns, the poet, balladeer, and Scotland's favorite son. "One of the very best Whisky Cocktails," writes Harry Craddock in *The Savoy Cocktail Book*. "A very fast mover on Saint Andrew's Day." Tradition holds that a shortbread cookie is served on the side.

> 2 ounces Scotch whiskey
> 1 ounce Italian vermouth
> 3 dashes Bénédictine

Combine ingredients in a mixing glass filled with cracked ice. Stir briskly and strain into a cocktail glass. Serve with a shortbread cookies.

Chancellor

Artifact of the late 19th or early 20th century, the Chancellor is a sibling of the Rob Roy, the Scotch Manhattan, adding fruit-forward Ruby Port, and swapping Dry Vermouth for Sweet. Scotch is called Scotch everywhere else but Scotland – there it is merely referred to as whisky. The cocktail's name refers to the presiding officer of the Scottish Parliament. "If a dryer drink is wanted," wrote Charles Browne, "the use of French Vermouth is allowable but is not orthodox."

> 2 ounces Scotch whiskey
> 1 ounce ruby port
> 1/2 ounce French vermouth
> 2 dashes orange bitters
> Orange peel, for garnish

Combine ingredients in a mixing glass filled with cracked ice. Stir briskly and strain into a cocktail glass. Express orange peel over the glass, rub around the rim, and drop in.

Up-to-Date

Hugo Ensslin, head bartender at the Hotel Wallick in New York City, is credited with being the first to record recipes for a few classic cocktails, including the "Manhattan-esque" Up-to-Date in 1916's *Recipes for Mixed Drinks*, billed as "a complete list of the standard mixed drinks that are in use at present in New York City."

> 2 dashes Grand Marnier
> 2 dashes Angostura bitters
> 1 ounce Sherry
> 1 ounce Canadian Club whisky

Combine ingredients in a mixing glass filled with cracked ice. Stir briskly and strain into a cocktail glass.

Brown University Cocktail

A simple, equal-parts Bourbon and Dry Vermouth drink, the Rosemary Cocktail (dating to Mark Twain's "Gilded Age") was animated with a smidgen of orange bitters, courtesy of the Ivy Leaguers up in Providence – for good reason. That one seemingly subtle addition brings about an entirely different cocktail, not only in name but in taste. (For the Harvard version, switch to Cognac and Sweet Vermouth).

> 1 1/2 ounces bourbon whiskey
> 1 1/2 ounces French vermouth
> 2 dashes orange bitters

Combine ingredients in a mixing glass filled with cracked ice. Stir briskly and strain into a cocktail glass.

Waldorf

It's one of the signature drinks of the original Waldorf, William Waldorf Astor's 13-story luxury hotel, opened in 1893 at the corner of Fifth Avenue and 33rd Street. In his *The Old Waldorf-Astoria Bar Book*, A.S. Crockett calls for equal parts of Whiskey, Vermouth and Absinthe (too much Absinthe for most tastes, so the recipe was modified over the years).

> 1/4 ounce absinthe, for rinse
> 2 ounces rye whiskey
> 3/4 ounce Italian vermouth
> 2 dashes Angostura bitters

Rinse a cocktail coupe glass with Absinthe and discard the excess. Combine remaining ingredients in a mixing glass filled with cracked ice. Stir briskly until chilled and diluted and strain into the prepared glass.

Palmetto

While nearly all early versions of the Manhattan were whiskey-centric, white-jacketed Harry Craddock, one of the most influential bartenders of the early-20th century, took a different path with the Palmetto, first appearing in *The Savoy Cocktail Book*. When Harry Craddock was asked about the proper way to consume a cocktail, he said, "Quickly. While it's still laughing at you."

> 1 1/2 ounces rum
> 1 1/2 ounces Italian vermouth
> 2 dashes orange bitters
> orange peel

Combine ingredients in a mixing glass filled with cracked ice. Stir briskly and strain into a cocktail glass. Express orange peel over the glass, rub around the rim, and drop in.

SCOFFLAW

In 1923 Delcevare King, a supporter of Prohibition announced a $200 prize to anyone who created a term that best expressed "the idea of lawless drinker, menace, bad citizen." Over 25,000 entries later, "scofflaw" was the winner, and the following year a bartender known only as "Jock," debuted his cocktail recipe at Harry's Bar in Paris. Poking fun at the folly of the American Prohibition, he called it the Scofflaw Cocktail. The formula first appeared in Patrick Gavin Duffy's 1934 *Official Mixer's Manual*. (Originally the Scofflaw was made with Canadian Whiskey, since production American Rye Whiskey ceased during Prohibition).

> 1 1/2 ounces rye whiskey
> 1 ounce French vermouth
> 3/4 ounce lemon juice, freshly squeezed
> 3/4 ounce grenadine syrup
> 2 dashes orange bitters
> lemon peel

Combine ingredients in a mixing glass filled with cracked ice. Shake vigorously and strain into a cocktail glass. Express lemon peel over the glass, rub around the rim, and drop in.

Marconi Wireless

It is said that the twentieth century didn't truly begin until December 12, 1901, when inventor Guglielmo Marconi, succeeded in transmitting radio signals across the Atlantic. This recipe, essentially an Apple Brandy Manhattan, was supposedly named after the wireless genius himself, according to the *Old Waldorf-Astoria Bar Book*, on his visit to the hotel.

> 2 ounces Laird's Applejack
> 1 ounce Italian vermouth
> 2 dashes orange bitters
> orange peel

Combine ingredients in a mixing glass filled with cracked ice. Stir briskly and strain into a cocktail glass. Express orange peel over the glass, rub around the rim, and drop in.

Algonquin

The Algonquin Hotel on 44th Street in New York City was headquarters to the legendary "Round Table," whose members included the likes of Dorothy Parker, Robert Benchley, George S. Kaufman, and Harpo Marx. They would gather for lunch, sip cocktails, exchange barbs, stories, anecdotes, and what have you – Prohibition be damned. In this liquid homage, the brawny shoulders of Rye keep sweetness of the pineapple in check – and vice-versa.

> 1 1/2 ounces rye whiskey
> 3/4 ounce French vermouth
> 3/4 ounce pineapple juice

Combine ingredients in a mixing glass filled with cracked ice. Stir briskly and strain into a cocktail glass.

Remember the Maine

After the sinking of the Maine, a U.S. naval ship, off the coast of Havana in 1898, war-mongering journalists used the phrase "Remember the Maine, to Hell with Spain" as a rallying cry that would jumpstart the Spanish-American War. "Treat this one with the respect it deserves, gentlemen," writes Charles H. Baker in his 1939 classic, *The Gentleman's Companion, or Around the World with Jigger, Beaker and Flask.* "Stir briskly in clock-wise fashion – this makes it sea-going, presumably!"

>   1/4 ounce absinthe
>   2 ounces rye whiskey
>   3/4 ounce Italian vermouth
>   2 teaspoons Cherry Heering
>   brandied cherry

Rinse a cocktail coupe glass with Absinthe and discard the excess. Combine remaining ingredients in a mixing glass filled with cracked ice. Stir briskly until chilled and diluted and strain into the prepared glass. Garnish with cherry.

Stork Club Manhattan

After World War II, when New York City was the epicenter of American culture and the Stork Club was a key New York social institution, Lucius Beebe, author of *The Stork Club Bar Book*, wrote, "The most exciting Manhattan is one compounded with ordinary quality bar whiskey rather than the rarest overproof article. It is perhaps the only mixed drink where this generality obtains."

>   2/3 ounce rye whiskey
>   1/3 ounce Italian vermouth

Combine ingredients in a mixing glass filled with cracked ice. Stir briskly and strain into a into a cocktail glass.

THE BRONX TWO-STEP

Nick: Oh, honey...
Nora: I'll be with you in two shakes of a cocktail.
Nick: Cocktail? Cocktail? I think I'll try one of those things.

At the turn of the century when the five boroughs were consolidated into one city, the large parcel of land north of Manhattan was owned by a wealthy family named Broncks. When city dwellers wanted to escape suburbia, they went up to the Broncks' estate. The spelling of the only borough of New York City that isn't an island was eventually changed to Bronx.

Scott Fitzgerald included the Bronx cocktail in his 1920 classic novel *This Side of Paradise*, where it factors in a rather drunken evening for protagonist Amory Blaine. He's at the old Knickerbocker Bar in New York, drowning his sorrows after a romantic breakup, and having more than a few belts with some fellow Princetonians. He's drinking Bronxes, "his head spinning gorgeously, layer upon layer of soft satisfaction setting over the bruised spots of his spirit."

Reporter: Say listen, is Nick working on a case?
Nora: Yes, yes!
Reporter: What case?
Nora: A case of scotch. Pitch in and help him.

The Bronx

The Bronx Cocktail is essentially a "Perfect" Martini with a complement of orange juice. Long neglected but certainly not forgotten, the Bronx was second only to the Martini and the Manhattan in the Nick and Nora era. The original recipe is attributed to Johnnie Solon, a bartender at the Waldorf-Astoria, after being challenged by a customer to come up with a new drink, one he named after the newly-opened Bronx zoo. It was the first drink to make the addition of fruit juice to a cocktail acceptable, and soon after, the hotel was going through a case of oranges a day.

> 1 1/2 ounces gin
> 3/4 ounce French vermouth
> 3/4 ounce Italian vermouth
> 1 ounce orange juice
> orange peel

Combine ingredients in a mixing glass filled with cracked ice. Stir briskly and strain into a chilled cocktail coupe glass. Express orange peel over the glass, rub around the rim, and drop in.

Boothby's Bronx Cocktail

In 1891, this version of the Bronx was published in *Cocktail Boothby's American Bartender* by William Thomas Boothby, the San Francisco bartender who was, in the years before Prohibition, the dean of West Coast mixologists. Orange Bitters provide a bright, citrusy depth that enhances Mr. Boothby's Bronx.

> 1 ounce gin
> 1 ounce Italian vermouth
> 1 ounce French vermouth
> 1 barspoon orange juice
> 2 dashes orange bitters
> orange peel

Combine ingredients in a mixing glass filled with cracked ice. Stir briskly and strain into a coupe glass. Express orange peel over the glass, rub around the rim, and drop in.

Silver Bronx

Before the onset of Prohibition, the last legal cocktail in America is said to have been mixed at the old Holland House on New York's Fifth Avenue by Harry Craddock, one of the most influential mixologists of the early-20th century. Before he set off for London to resume tending bar at the Savoy Hotel, Mr. Craddock created a "Silver" version of the Bronx for publication in *The Savoy Cocktail Book*.

> 2 ounces gin
> 1 ounce orange juice
> 1 dash French vermouth
> 1 dash Italian vermouth
> 1 egg white
> orange peel

Combine ingredients in a mixing glass filled with cracked ice. Shake vigorously and strain into a coupe glass. Express orange peel over the glass, rub around the rim, and drop in.

Income Tax Cocktail

The earliest published recipe is Harry Craddock's 1930 *Savoy Cocktail Book,* which shows it to be essentially a Bronx with a couple dashes of bitters. Given how hard it is to get the flavors of the Bronx to hold together as a cohesive drink, adding bitters must have seemed a natural embellishment, probably tried in many places at many times. Somewhere along the way, someone gave it the name "Income Tax," perhaps a wink and a nod to the "bitterness" of tax season.

> 1 1/2 ounces gin
> 3/4 ounce dry vermouth
> 3/4 ounce sweet vermouth
> Juice of 1/4 orange
> 2 dashes Angostura bitters
> orange peel

Combine liquid ingredients in a mixing glass filled with cracked ice. Shake vigorously and strain into a cocktail glass. Express orange peel over the glass, rub around the rim, and drop in.

Satan's Whiskers

The cocktail emerged from the Embassy Club, a Hollywood speakeasy run by impresario Adolph "Eddie" Brandstatter. It is said that wherever Eddie was, that was the party. Satan's Whiskers is a variation on the Bronx, first appearing in print in Harry Craddock's *Savoy Cocktail Book* from 1930. (The drink can be made in two ways – either "straight" with Grand Marnier, or "curled" with Orange Curaçao).

> 1/2 ounce gin
> 1/2 ounce Grand Marnier
> 1/2 ounce Italian vermouth
> 1/2 ounce French vermouth
> 1/2 ounce orange juice
> 1 dash orange bitters
> orange peel

Combine ingredients in a mixing glass filled with cracked ice. Shake and strain into a Martini glass. Express orange peel over the glass, rub around the rim, and drop in.

Queens Cocktail

A variation of the Bronx with a nod to another borough, the Queens Cocktail substitutes pineapple juice for orange juice, once again the brainstorm of Mr. Harry Craddock during huis tenure at the American Bar in London's Savoy Hotel. Harry is considered one of the most influential bartenders of the early 20th century.

> 1 1/2 ounces gin
> 1 ounce pineapple juice
> 3/4 ounce Italian vermouth
> 3/4 ounce French vermouth
> orange peel

Combine liquid ingredients in a mixing glass filled with cracked ice. Shake vigorously and strain into a cocktail glass. Express orange peel over the glass, rub around the rim, and drop in.

THE MARTINI WALTZ

Nora (suffering from a hangover): What hit me?
Nick: The last Martini. How 'bout a pick-me-up
Nora: No!

"The Martini is civilized, expressive of communal relations," insists Paul Manning in *Semiotics of Drink and Drinking*, "on the other hand, since it is very nearly pure gin, it is associated with destructive excess; the ritual of drinking it together celebrates communality and egalitarian relationships, in the case of Nick and Nora Charles particularly."

Since its inception at the Knickerbocker Bar, you could say the Martini has become half drink, half art form, combining energy and austerity, power and subtlety, urbanity and sophistication, as bartenders have continued to experiment with ways to refine and reinterpret the timeless formula.

The Thin Man is one of the first appearances of the Martini specifically "shaken, not stirred," according to Nick Charles himself.

Nora: How many drinks have you had?
Nick: This will make six Martinis.
Nora (to the waiter): All right. Will you bring me five more Martinis, Leo?
Line them right up here.

Martini Cocktail

For the Martini likely sipped by Nick and Nora, we refer to Harry McElhone, a defining figure in early 20th-century bartending, most famous for his role at Harry's New York Bar in Paris, which he bought in 1923. He worked at Ciro's Club in Deauville and the Plaza Hotel New York, and is credited with inventing many cocktails, including the Bloody Mary, Sidecar, the Monkey Gland, the White Lady, and an early form of the Martini, as published in 1927's *Barflies and Cocktails*.

> 2 ounces dry gin
> 1 ounce French vermouth
> 1 dash orange bitters

Combine ingredients in a mixing glass filled with cracked ice. Shake well and strain into a cocktail glass.

Martinez

The Martini's earliest incarnation was shaped with Old Tom Gin, a botanically-intensive style, rounded by light sweetness. (Its interaction with Sweet Vermouth and Maraschino actually suggests a kinship with the Manhattan Cocktail). According to John Walker's *Bottoms Up: Being a Glossary of Useful Information for the Thirsty* (1928), George Rector's Hotel Claridge in New York City was a "turbulent rendezvous for the disciples of the Martinez."

> 1 1/2 ounces Old Tom gin
> 1 1/2 ounces Italian vermouth
> 1 dash Angostura bitters
> 2 dashes Maraschino liqueur
> lemon peel

Combine ingredients in a mixing glass filled with cracked ice. Stir briskly and strain into a cocktail coupe glass. Express lemon peel over the glass, rub around the rim, and drop in.

Abbey Martini

President of the United Kingdom Bartender's Guild, William J. Tarling compiled *The Cafe Royal Cocktail Book*, one of the literary gems of the gilded age of cocktails. Cafe Royal was a place where American spirits mixed with European liqueurs and aperitifs in astounding ways, reflecting the glamor and decadence of pre-war England. Tarling's Abbey Martini is closely related to the better-known Bronx. Angostura bitters help balance the drink and add an extra burst of flavor.

> 2 ounces dry gin
> 1 ounce Lillet
> 1 ounce orange juice, fresh
> 3 dashes Angostura bitters
> orange peel

Combine liquid ingredients in a mixing glass filled with cracked ice. Stir briskly and strain into a coupe glass. Express orange peel over the glass, rub around the rim, and drop in.

Gin and It

Bon vivant Charles H. Baker, who ate and drank his way around the world in the first quarter of the 20th century, chronicled his adventure in the two-volume *Gentleman's Companion*. In it, he succinctly described the importance of Gin: "No bar can be without dry gin and be called a bar." The "It" in this minimalist recipe is Sweet (Italian) Vermouth, "the wetter the better." Traditionally, no ice is used in this drink. The libation is sometimes called Gin and Cin (pronounced "sin") after Cinzano, a popular brand of Italian Sweet Vermouth. Traditionally, no ice is used in this drink, however, if you do mix over ice and add a dash of Orange Bitters, you'll have yourself a Yale Cocktail.

   1 1/2 ounces gin
   1 1/2 ounces Italian vermouth

Combine ingredients in a mixing glass without ice. Stir and strain into a coupe glass.

Zaza

A play by French playwrights Pierre Berton and Charles Simon, *Zaza* was produced in America in 1898 adaptation by David Belasco. The title character is a prostitute who becomes a music hall entertainer and the mistress of a married man. *Zaza* captured the imagination of New York bartender Hugo Ensslin who included this appreciation in 1916's *Recipes for Mixed Drinks*.

> 1 1/2 ounces gin
> 1 1/2 ounces Dubonnet Rouge
> 1 dash Angostura bitters
> lemon peel

Combine ingredients in a mixing glass filled with cracked ice. Stir briskly and strain into a cocktail coupe glass. Express lemon peel over the glass, rub around the rim, and drop in.

Hanky-Panky

The American Bar at London's Savoy Hotel was one of the early establishments to introduce American-style cocktails to Europe. Ada "Coley" Coleman became head bartender, where, during the 1920s, she mixed potions for the likes of Mark Twain, the Prince of Wales, Prince Wilhelm of Sweden, and Sir Charles Hawtrey. It was Hawtrey, Britain's leading comedy actor of the era, for whom Coleman created the Hanky-Panky Cocktail.

    1 1/2 ounces gin
    1 1/2 ounces Italian vermouth
    2 dashes Fernet Branca
    orange peel

Combine ingredients in a mixing glass filled with cracked ice. Stir briskly and strain into a cocktail coupe glass. Express orange peel over the glass, rub around the rim, and drop in.

The Barry Cocktail

There's a strong tie between the Barry and other flirtations with the Martini formula during Prohibition, this version distinguished by a hint of mint. In 1929, Charles H. Baker Jr. first met "Barry" at the Army & Navy Club in Manila, Philippines. Like all proper Martinis, according to Mr. Baker, the drink "must be cold indeed."

> 2 ounces gin
> 1 ounce Italian vermouth
> 1 dash Angostura bitters
> 1/2 teaspoon white crème de menthe

Add gin, vermouth, and bitters to a mixing glass filled with cracked ice. Stir briskly and strain into a chilled cocktail coupe glass. Float crème de menthe by holding a teaspoon bottom-side up over the glass and pouring the liqueur slowly over it.

Colony Cocktail

The Colony, rendezvous of New York high society, remained open through the "dry" years of Prohibition, hiding the liquor stash in an elevator as a precaution against raids by enforcement agents. Marco Hattem, the Colony's head bartender, is credited with not only devising the house cocktail, but, while stirring Martinis was the nearly universal custom, he made a practice of shaking them vigorously.

> 1 1/2 ounce gin
> 3/4 ounce grapefruit juice
> 2 teaspoon Maraschino liqueur

Combine ingredients in a mixing glass filled with cracked ice. Stir briskly and strain into a cocktail coupe glass.

COOPERSTOWN

In *The Stork Club Bar Book*, Lucius Beebe imbeds this drink among the "less exotic but nonetheless popular noontime cocktails" served at the bar, a "perfect" version of the Martini, using equal parts of both Sweet and Dry Vermouth. Skip the mint and add a shot of Cognac for an Astor Painless Anesthetic, the Stork's hangover cure, devised by actress Mary Astor (Brigid O'Shaughnessy in *The Maltese Falcon*).

> 1 1/2 ounces gin
> 1/2 ounce French vermouth
> 1/2 ounce Italian vermouth
> 2 sprigs fresh mint

Combine ingredients in a mixing glass filled with cracked ice. Shake and strain into a Martini glass. Garnish with mint sprigs.

Cornell Cocktail

In *The Old Waldorf-Astoria Bar Book*, Albert Crockett calls this drink "a compliment to an institution at Ithaca, many of whose alumni – mining engineers and others – used it to toast Alma Mater." If you splash in some orange bitters, the Cornell becomes a Dewey; if you add a squeeze of orange peel to a Dewey, you've got a Racquet Club, which, with Italian vermouth and a dash of Angostura, answers to the name of Hearst.

> 1 1/2 ounces gin
> 1 1/2 ounces French vermouth

Combine ingredients in a mixing glass filled with cracked ice. Stir briskly and strain into a coupe glass.

Gibson

Improvised by bartender Charley Connolly of the Players Club for "Gibson Girl" illustrator Charles Dana Gibson, the Gibson Cocktail lends a whisper of savory and umami undertone to the Martini with a pickled cocktail onion in place of the typical briny olive. In 1957, *Esquire Magazine* compiled a list of celebrity thirst quenchers in *Drink Book*, including this onion-laden Gibson courtesy of Guy Lombardo, whose orchestra played at the Roosevelt Hotel in New York City.

> **2 ounces gin**
> **1/2 ounce French vermouth**
> **6 pearl onions**

Combine liquid ingredients in a mixing glass filled with cracked ice. Stir briskly and strain into a Martini glass. Drop onions into the glass.

Gin Cocktail

According to a New York columnist, barman "Oscar Haimo measures, pours, stirs, or shakes, as the case may be, the ingredients as if he were presiding at the discovery and birth of some new chemical process which will stir the soul of all mankind." During his service at the Pierre Hotel, Mr. Haimo published a version of Pink Gin in *Cocktail Digest*. Angostura adds a bright red color and a lovely aromatic blanket to the drink.

> **2 1/2 ounces gin**
> **2 dashes Angostura bitters**

Combine gin and Angostura bitters in a mixing glass filled with cracked ice. Stir briskly and strain into a cocktail glass.

The Crisp

John Applegreen, who performed bartending duties at Kinsley's in Chicago and later at the Holland House in New York, advanced the concept of a "Dry Martini," inspired not by ingredient proportions, but with the emergence of the London Dry gin style. The Crisp Cocktail made its first appeared in the 1899 edition of *Applegreen's Bar Book*. He believed the drink should neither taste solely of gin nor vermouth; it ought to be a perfect balance of both.

> **1 3/4 ounces dry gin**
> **1 3/4 ounces French vermouth**
> **2 dashes orange bitters**
> **lemon peel**

Combine liquid ingredients in a mixing glass filled with cracked ice. Stir briskly and strain into a coupe glass. Express lemon peel over the glass, rub around the rim, and drop in.

The McCutcheon

Among the "invigorators and brain dusters" in *Applegreen's Bar Book*, the McCutcheon cocktail begins where the Crisp Cocktail left off, marrying gin with both sweet and dry vermouths, then christening the drink with the persistent cherry aromatics of Maraschino, one of the oldest European liqueurs.

- 1 1/2 ounces dry gin
- 3/4 ounce French vermouth
- 3/4 ounce Italian vermouth
- 1 dash Maraschino liqueur
- 1 dash orange bitters

Combine ingredients in a mixing glass filled with cracked ice. Stir briskly and strain into a coupe glass.

Astoria

Its name inspired by John Jacob Astor, the era's wealthiest American, the Astoria was conceived by Jacques Straub, manager of the famed Pendennis Club of Louisville, Kentucky, later the wine steward of the Blackstone Hotel in Chicago. In 1914, Straub authored a collection of recipes called *Drinks*, and the Astoria appears among its 700 recipes. His use of Old Tom gin instead of London dry added sweetness and a softer, mellower quality to the cocktail.

> **2 ounces Old Tom gin**
> **1 ounce French vermouth**
> **dash of orange bitters**
> **lemon peel**

Combine liquid ingredients in a mixing glass filled with cracked ice. Stir briskly and strain into a chilled coupe glass. Express lemon peel over the glass, rub around the rim, and drop in.

Turf Club

A sibling of the Martinez was first concocted at New York's Turf Club, the gentlemen's club on the corner of Madison Avenue and 26th Street, where members gathered to play the horses. Albert Stevens Crockett immortalized the thirst quencher in The Waldorf-Astoria Bar Book, writing, "At times a good half – possibly two-thirds – of the crowd in the bar were interested in racing, and would appreciate a cocktail of such a name."

> **2 ounces Holland Gin (Genever)**
> **1 ounce Italian vermouth**
> **1 dash Angostura bitters**
> **lemon peel**

Combine ingredients in a mixing glass filled with cracked ice. Stir briskly and strain into a cocktail coupe glass. Express lemon peel over the glass, rub around the rim, and drop in.

Heyday of the Cocktail

Nora (after Nick gets shot at): Do you want a drink?
Nick: What do you think?

December 5th, 1933. This was the day that Prohibition, otherwise known as the Great Experiment, ended and America was free to consume alcohol once again. Everyone was ready for a little cheer, and Nick and Nora Charles were the ones to throw the party.

With Repeal, well-made cocktails burst back on the scene, retaining their mystique and acquiring new glamour on the silver screen, as Nick and Nora spread the liquid gospel.

The best cocktails, revived and renewed during the Nick and Nora era, have been infused into our popular, historical and literary culture, often becoming as iconic as the man and woman who drank them.

Nick: Can't you get to sleep?
Nora: No.
Nick: Well, maybe you should take a drink. It will help you.
Nora: No, thanks.
Nick: Well, then maybe it will help if I took it!

Monkey Gland

Dr. Serge Voronoff, a French surgeon of Russian extraction, gained more than a small amount of fame and fortune for implanting the testicles of monkeys into men for alleged aphrodisiac effects. He went from being highly respected to a subject of ridicule, his procedure immortalized by the "Monkey Doodle Doo" song in the Marx Brothers film *The Cocoanuts* which includes the lyrics, "If you're too old for dancing, get yourself a monkey gland"). Bartender Frank Meier named an "awful wallop" of a cocktail at the Ritz in "honor" of Dr. Voronoff.

> 1 1/2 ounces gin
> 1 1/2 ounces orange juice
> 1 dash Pernod
> 1 dash grenadine syrup

Combine ingredients in a mixing glass filled with cracked ice. Shake vigorously and strain into a cocktail glass.

Maiden's Blush

"They talk about Prohibition in America. What can one do in a country such as that? What does one do in America when one is sad – without alcohol," contemplates Joseph Roth in 1924's *Hotel Savoy*. Harry Craddock, the hotel's bartender, is often given credit for this drink, its bright pink color brought on by the grenadine, the color of a young dame's cheek. The coy cocktail (according to A. J. Rathbun) is "a mixture surely fit for most maiden's a-blushing."

> 1 1/2 ounces Gin
> 3/4 ounce Pernod
> 1/2 barspoon grenadine syrup

Combine ingredients in a mixing glass filled with cracked ice. Shake vigorously and strain into a cocktail glass.

Champagne Cocktail

Back in the glory days, high-spirited ladies of the music hall had a penchant for Champagne, and this "improved cocktail," subbing bubbly for spirit in a mix that includes aromatic bitters, became known as "Chorus Girls Milk," a delightful nod to decadence. "Champagne is the ebullient ambassador with plenary powers at the Court of Ebriety," writes Crosby Gaige in his 1941 *Cocktail Guide and Ladies Companion.*

- 1 sugar cube
- Angostura bitters
- Champagne
- Lemon peel

Soak the sugar cube in Angostura bitters and drop into a coupe glass. Top up with Champagne. Express lemon peel over the glass, rub around the rim, and drop in.

Widow's Kiss

Created by George Kappeler at New York's Holland House Hotel, this well-matched set of ingredients disappeared into the vacuum of Prohibition. Ted Haigh, the inimitable Dr. Cocktail, compares the taste of the Widow's Kiss to the feeling of finding in a dusty attic old love letters wrapped in lace in your grandmother's 1914 suitcase.

> 1 1/2 ounces Calvados
> 3/4 ounce Yellow Chartreuse
> 3/4 ounce Benedictine
> 2 dashes Angostura bitters
> brandied cherry

Combine liquid ingredients in a mixing glass filled with cracked ice. Stir briskly and strain into a cocktail glass. Drop cherry into the glass.

Bosom Caresser

The drink was concocted by Harry Craddock at the American Bar in London's Savoy Hotel. According to Craddock, "the drink might be called Bobby Jones or the Francis Ouimet Cocktail, as these two gentleman golfers, usually so chary of expressing preferences, distinctly expressed one for this concoction."

    1 1/2 ounces brandy
    1 1/2 ounces Madeira
    1 egg yolk
    1 dash Cointreau
    1 dash grenadine syrup

Combine liquid ingredients in a mixing glass filled with cracked ice. Shake vigorously and strain into a cocktail glass.

Buck's Fizz

Captain H. J. Buckmaster of the Royal Horse Guards established the Buck's Club, a venerable gentlemen's club in London in 1919 (whose membership included Winston Churchill). The Buck's Fizz was concocted in 1921 by barman Malachy "Pat" MacGarry at the club's American Cocktail Bar, a less stuffy and more convivial gathering place than had previously existed in British gentlemen's clubs.

orange juice, chilled
Champagne, chilled

Fill a coupe glass 2/3 full of orange juice. Top up with Champagne.

Mary Pickford

During Prohibition, Havana was Mecca for thirsty Americans and the luxurious Gran Hotel Sevilla (later called the Sevilla Biltmore), whose elegant, air-conditioned bar was decorated by famous Cuban caricaturist Conrado Massager, became the social center of Havana. During his stint at the Sevilla, barman Eddie Woelke created this Daiquiri variant in honor of "America's Sweetheart," silent screen actress Mary Pickford.

> **2 ounces rum**
> **2 ounces unsweetened pineapple juice**
> **1/2 teaspoon grenadine syrup**

Combine ingredients in a mixing glass filled with cracked ice. Shake vigorously and strain into a coupe glass.

Ace of Clubs

The Ace of Clubs Lounge on Front Street and the corner of Parliament in Hamilton, Bermuda, attracted American tourists during the 1930s. The house cocktail was a twist on the Daiquiri, preserved in the pages of *Esquire Magazine*. Crème de cacao gives it an intriguing depth of flavor without dominating the mix.

> **2 ounces rum**
> **1/2 ounce white crème de cacao**
> **1/2 ounce lime juice**
> **1/2 teaspoon simple syrup**

Combine ingredients in a mixing glass filled with cracked ice. Shake vigorously and strain into a coupe glass.

Aviation

Created by Hugo Ensslin, head bartender at the Hotel Wallick in New York, and first published in Ensslin's 1916 *Recipes for Mixed Drinks*, the recipe is a variation on the Gin Sour, using Maraschino as sweetener. Although the drink originally called for a dash of Crème de Violette, the obscure liqueur was omitted in Harry Craddock's influential *Savoy Cocktail Book* (1930).

> **2 ounces gin**
> **2 teaspoons Maraschino liqueur**
> **3/4 ounce lemon juice, freshly squeezed**

Combine ingredients in a mixing glass filled with cracked ice. Shake vigorously and strain into a coupe glass.

Jack Rose

Its name is a play on words: the drink is made with Applejack and is rose-colored from the grenadine. (Applejack is a Calvados-style apple brandy, which has claims to being the oldest American spirit due to its roots in the colonial period). The fruity, spirit-forward drink appears in Ernest Hemingway's 1926 classic, *The Sun Also Rises*, in which Jake Barnes, the storyteller and protagonist, drinks a Jack Rose at the bar of the Hôtel de Crillon while awaiting the arrival of Lady Brett Ashley.

> **2 ounces Laird's Applejack**
> **1 ounce lemon juice, freshly squeezed**
> **1/2 ounce grenadine syrup**

Combine ingredients in a mixing glass filled with cracked ice. Shake vigorously and strain into a cocktail coupe glass.

Clover Club

Christened for the Philadelphia Men's Club whose members gathered at the Bellevue-Stratford Hotel, and according to the *Old Waldorf-Astoria Bar Book*, "dined and wined, and wined again." The Clover Club drinker was described by Jack Townsend, president of the Bartenders Union of New York and author of The Bartender's Book, as "traditionally a gentleman of the pre-Prohibition school," a "distinguished patron of the oak-paneled lounge."

> **2 ounces gin**
> **juice of 1/2 lemon**
> **1 teaspoon grenadine syrup**
> **1 egg white**

Combine ingredients in a mixing glass filled with cracked ice. Shake vigorously and strain into a small wine glass.

Southside Cocktail

Jack & Charlie's '21' was designed with its own disappearing bar and a secret cellar to hide the illegal liquor from prying eyes, and although the speakeasy was raided by police numerous times during Prohibition, not a drop of alcohol was ever found. The Southside Cocktail is said to have been invented at the Southside Sportsmen's Club on Long Island, then popularized by the '21' faithful. The cocktail is sometimes topped with Champagne to make a Southside Fizz.

> **2 ounces gin**
> **1 ounce lemon juice, freshly squeezed**
> **3/4 ounce simple syrup**
> **sprig of fresh mint**

Combine ingredients in a mixing glass filled with cracked ice. Shake vigorously and strain into a coupe glass. Garnish with a mint leaf.

Chicago Cocktail

Cocktail imbibing, finally legalized a year after the club opened, was practiced enthusiastically at Chicago's Chez Paree. It was *Chicago Daily News* reporter John Drury who provided the definitive recipe for the city's eponymous libation in his restaurant guide, Dining in Chicago, faithfully crafted in sugar-rimmed coupes by the club's white-jacketed barman Wellington Dent Campanelli, who everyone called "Duke Camp."

> **2 ounces brandy**
> **1/4 teaspoon triple sec**
> **1 dash Angostura bitters**
> **Champagne, chilled**
> **lemon peel**

Prepare a cocktail glass by rubbing a lemon slice around the rim and dipping it in powdered sugar. Combine the brandy, triple sec and bitters in mixing glass with cracked ice. Briefly shake and strain into the prepared glass. Top up with Champagne. Express lemon peel over the glass, rub around the rim, and drop in.

Harlem Cocktail

When Prohibition ended in 1933 and America was again allowed to drink legally, Charlie Conolly, head barman of the Player's Club, was hired to revamp the Cotton Club bar and create new cocktails. Booze, the main attraction rivaling the floor show, was cheap and plentiful. Offered for the first time, "fancy mixed drinks" included Sloe Gin Rickey, Silver Fizz, Sherry Flip, and the Harlem Cocktail, a Conolly original. Shake, strain into cocktail glass... and hey! hey!

> 1 1/2 ounces gin
> 3/4 ounce pineapple juice
> 1 barspoon Maraschino liqueur
> Maraschino cherry

Combine liquid ingredients in a mixing glass filled with cracked ice. Shake vigorously and strain into a cocktail glass. Garnish with Maraschino cherry.

Blue Moon

The New York City-invented cocktail was a favorite of the boys at Joel's Green Room, a 41st Street haunt for actors, artists and newspaper folk – before Mr. Volstead appeared. Slightly sweet and fragrant, Broadway columnist O.O. McIntyre called it "high powered in action." When booze was legal again, the Blue Moon found a new home at the Horseshoe's Silver Dollar Bar (upholstered with real silver dollars embedded in the floor).

> **2 ounces gin**
> **1/2 ounce crème de violette**
> **1/2 ounce freshly-squeezed lemon juice**
> **lemon peel**

Combine liquid ingredients in a mixing glass filled with cracked ice. Shake vigorously and strain into a coupe glass. Express lemon peel over the glass, rub around the rim, and drop in.

Horse's Neck

In the 1935 Fred Astaire-Ginger Rogers screwball musical comedy *Top Hat*, the glamorous Helen Broderick orders "un altro Horse's Neck" in a cinematically-stylized cocktail lounge. The highball became the latest craze among cocktail drinkers in the movie colony.

> 2 ounces blended whiskey
> ginger ale, chilled
> 3 dashes Angostura bitters

Fill a Collins glass with ice and add the whiskey. Top up with ginger ale. Add the bitters and gently stir with bar spoon.

Mamie Taylor

Legendary Leon and Eddie's was a raucous New York nightclub that didn't give a hoot about sophistication. A sign at the door was a takeoff on the famous Earl Carroll slogan and read "Through these portals, the most beautiful girls in the world pass out!" Popular with the heavy drinking crowd at Leon & Eddie's, the scotch-based Mamie Taylor was invented by a bartender in upstate Rochester and named after a turn-of-the-century opera singer. Put the blame on Mame!

> **2 ounces scotch**
> **1/2 ounce lime juice**
> **4 ounces ginger beer, chilled**
> **lime wedge**

Fill a large highball glass with ice. Add the scotch, ginger beer and lime juice. Gently stir. Garnish with lime wedge.

Monkey Wrench

Mike Connolly was the gossip columnist for *The Hollywood Reporter*. His favorite bartender was the Mocambo's Johnny Trebach, who playfully mispronounced Mike's name as "Cannoli" while keeping his cigarettes lighted and drinks refreshed. The Monkey Wrench, one of Trebach's specialties, was named for the adjustable pipe wrench.

> 1 1/2 ounces rum
> 3 ounces freshly-squeezed grapefruit juice
> 1 dash bitters

Combine ingredients in a mixing glass filled with cracked ice. Stir briskly and strain into a coupe glass.

The Puritan

By the turn of the last century, European and American palates were becoming accustomed to the refreshing dryness of the new, London-style gins. The Puritan, possibly so named for its dryness, appeared in Frederic Lawrence Knowles' 1900 *The Cocktail Book: A Sideboard Manual for Gentlemen*, a precursor to the Dry Martini.

> 1 1/2 ounce gin
> 3/4 ounce French vermouth
> 1 barspoon Yellow Chartreuse
> 3 dashes orange bitters

Combine ingredients in a mixing glass filled with cracked ice. Stir for 10 seconds and strain into a coupe glass.

Vanishing Cream

Crosby Gaige, once described as "Manhattan's authentically distinguished man-about-the-boulevards," recommended the addition of a cherry to this 1940s-era cream drink. "Never argue with a cherry or strike it in anger," cautioned Gaige.

> **2 ounces apricot brandy**
> **1 ounce fresh cream**
> **1 dash gin**
> **Maraschino cherry**

Combine ingredients in a mixing glass with cracked ice. Shake vigorously and strain into cocktail coupe glass. Drop cherry into the glass.

Glover's Mange Cure

"In the world of potables, the cocktail represents adventure and experiment," insists Crosby Gaige. "All other forms of drinking are more or less static." His 1941 *Cocktail Guide and Ladies Companion*, described as a serious study of the thoughts of the leading bartenders of his era, includes a mix of two of the more famous medicinal liqueurs invented by monks. "Shake, strain, and rub briskly into the tonsils," he suggests.

- 1/2 ounce Benedictine
- 1/2 ounce Green Chartreuse
- 1 ounce Laird's Applejack
- 1 dash Angostura bitters

Combine ingredients in a mixing glass filled with cracked ice. Shake vigorously and strain into a coupe glass.

Golden Slipper

This simple equation is put forward by Bill Kelly in his 1945 book, *The Roving Bartender*, the "little book for those who don't know and know they don't know." As a founding member of the B. I. L. (Bartenders International League), his motto was "Always remember to treat your brother bartenders with courtesy, and see that they treat you the same."

- 1 ounce Yellow Chartreuse
- 1 ounce brandy
- 1 egg yolk

Combine ingredients in a mixing glass filled with cracked ice. Shake vigorously and strain into a coupe glass.

Blackthorne Sour

Tom Bullock, the son of a former slave and Union soldier, served as bartender at the St. Louis Country Club and in 1917 was the first African-American to publish a cocktail manual. He dedicated *The Ideal Bartender* "To those who enjoy snug club rooms – that they may learn the art of preparing for themselves what is good." Important in the study of cocktail history, his book documents the early use of Chartreuse in mixed drinks.

> **1 ounce sloe gin**
> **1 barspoon pineapple juice**
> **1/2 barspoon Green Chartreuse**
> **4 dashes freshly-squeezed lime juice**
> **lime slice**
> **pineapple slice**

Combine liquid ingredients in a mixing glass filled with cracked ice. Stir for 10 seconds and strain into a cocktail glass. Garnish with fruit slices.

Xanthia

The sensual ménage à trois of gin, cherry brandy, and Yellow Chartreuse is herbal and fruity, its name derived from the Ancient Greek word Xanthos meaning "yellow," a reference to the yellow hue of the River Xanthos, colored by the soil in the alluvial base of the valley. The cocktail dates back at least to Harry McElhone's 1927 *Barflies and Cocktails*.

1 ounce gin
1 ounce kirsch
1 ounce Yellow Chartreuse

Combine ingredients in a mixing glass filled with cracked ice. Stir for 10 seconds and strain into a cocktail glass.

Yellow Parrot

"To millions and millions of people all over the world the Stork symbolizes and epitomizes the deluxe upholstery of quintessentially urban existence," pronounced society columnist Lucius Beebe. "It means fame; it means wealth; it means an elegant way of life among celebrated folk." This ménage à trois was created in 1935 by barman Albert Coleman at New York's legendary Stork Club.

> 1 ounce Yellow Chartreuse
> 1 ounce Pernod
> 1 ounce apricot brandy

Combine ingredients in a mixing glass filled with cracked ice. Stir for 10 seconds, and strain into a cocktail glass.

Warday's Cocktail

As transatlantic travel became more popular in the late 19th and early 20th centuries, many American-style bars opened throughout London. Warday himself was likely one of barman Harry Craddock's favored customers at the Savoy Hotel's American Bar, and his preferred sipper was this herbaceous, yet elegant blend of gin, Calvados, sweet vermouth, and Yellow Chartreuse – immortalized in Craddock's *Savoy Cocktail Book*.

> 1 ounce gin
> 1 ounce Calvados
> 1 ounce Italian vermouth
> 1 barspoon Green Chartreuse
> lemon peel

Combine ingredients in a mixing glass filled with cracked ice. Stir for 10 seconds and strain into a coupe glass. Express lime peel over the glass, rub around the rim, and drop in.

Fifth Avenue

Before the onset of Prohibition, the last legal cocktail in America is said to have been mixed at the old Holland House on New York's Fifth Avenue by Harry Craddock, one of the most influential mixologists of the early-20th century. Before he set off for London to resume tending bar at the Savoy Hotel, Mr. Craddock created a bracing libation, immortalized in the *Esquire Drink Book*, and named for its birthplace.

> 1 1/2 ounces gin
> 3/4 ounce Italian vermouth
> 3/4 ounce Fernet-Branca

Combine ingredients in a mixing glass filled with cracked ice. Shake vigorously and strain into a cocktail glass.

Don't Give Up the Ship

According to "Luscious" Lucius Beebe (moniker bestowed by Walter Winchell), Crosby Gaige was never known to shy away "when the ice in the shaker called stirringly to duty." His eccentric gin-based cocktail, invigorated with whispers of flavors and aromatics, is offered in Mr. Gaige's 1941 *Cocktail Guide and Ladies Companion*, described as a serious study of the thoughts of the leading bartenders of his era.

>1 1/2 ounces gin
>1 dash Fernet-Branca
>1 dash orange curacao
>1 dash Dubonnet Rouge
>lemon peel

Combine liquid ingredients in a mixing glass filled with cracked ice. Shake vigorously and strain into a cocktail glass. Express lemon peel over the glass, rub around the rim, and drop in.

Napoleon

"Glory is fleeting," said Napoléon Bonaparte, "but obscurity is forever." Italian barmen have revived this forgotten relic from Harry Craddock's 1930 *Savoy Cocktail Book*, enhancing the pleasant bitterness of wine-based Dubonnet with an adventurous dash of Fernet-Branca. Dubonnet was popularized during World War I by the British Queen Mother who sipped Craddock's Zaza Cocktail (Dubonnet and gin) every day at lunch.

> **2 ounces gin**
> **1/4 ounce Dubonnet Rouge**
> **1 ounce orange curacao**
> **1 dash Fernet-Branca**
> **lemon peel**

Combine liquid ingredients in a mixing glass filled with cracked ice. Stir for 10 seconds and strain into a cocktail glass. Express lemon peel over the glass, rub around the rim, and drop in.

KING COLE

The Old Fashioned had already become one of the era's essential cocktails when the King Cole made an appearance in Hugo Ensslin's 1916 *Recipes for Mixed Drinks*. Described as fit for "a merry old soul," his riff on the original substitutes Fernet-Branca for Angostura and includes fragrant pineapple in the muddled fruit. About muddling, Charles Browne (*Gun Club Drink Book*) wrote, "It does seem rather a rude way to treat good whiskey, but the ladies seem to like it."

> **fresh orange slice**
> **fresh pineapple chunk**
> **1/2 teaspoon powdered sugar**
> **2 dashed Fernet-Branca**
> **2 ounces rye whiskey**

Muddle orange slice, pineapple slice, and powdered sugar in an Old Fashioned glass. Add whiskey, Fernet-Branca, and 2 ice cubes. Stir to chill.

Fanciulli

An Italiano ispirato rendering of the Manhattan Cocktail formula, the drink first appeared in Albert Stevens Crockett's 1931 *Old Waldorf Bar Days*, named after Francesco "The Professor" Fanciulli, an Italian immigrant who enjoyed success composing comic operas before becoming leader of the U.S. Marine Corps band. Devotees usually took it without ice or garnish.

- 1 1/2 ounce bourbon
- 3/4 ounce Italian vermouth
- 3/4 ounce Fernet-Branca

Combine ingredients in a mixing glass filled with cracked ice. Stir for 10 seconds and strain into a cocktail glass.

Savoy Corpse Reviver

Among the family of restorative cocktails intended as "hair of the dog" hangover cures, the most memorable are the cognac- and gin-based Corpse Reviver and Corpse Reviver #2 cocktails listed in *The Savoy Cocktail Book* by Harry Craddock. The barman's advice: "to be taken before 11 AM, or whenever steam and energy are needed."

- 1 ounce brandy
- 1 ounce Fernet-Branca
- 1 ounce white crème de menthe

Combine ingredients in a mixing glass filled with cracked ice. Shake vigorously and strain into a small cocktail glass.

IBF Pick-Me-Up

Members of the International Bar Flies (IBF), founded in 1924 by O. O. McIntyre at Harry's New York Bar in Paris, have included Ernest Hemingway, Scott Fitzgerald, George Gershwin, Sinclair Lewis, Franklin Roosevelt, Gene Kelly, Noel Coward, Thornton Wilder, Marlene Dietrich, and many more. Legendary bartender Harry McElhone created this communal eye-opener for an organization devoted to "the uplift and downfall of serious drinkers."

> 2 ounces Cognac
> 2 dashes Fernet-Branca
> 2 dashes Cointreau
> Champagne, chilled

Combine ingredients (except Champagne) in a mixing glass filled with cracked ice. Shake vigorously and strain into a white wine glass. Top up with Champagne.

Toronto

First mentioned in 1922's *Cocktails: How to Make Them*, author Robert Vermiere notes, "this cocktail is much appreciated by the Canadians of Toronto." Likely created to highlight the mellow tones of Canadian whiskey, as well as appeal to Italian immigrants who arrived in Toronto during the 1920s, Fernet-Branca's complex, herbal aromatics add just the right amount of bite and dimension to the drink, while allowing earthy notes of the rye to peek through. Orange zest brighten up an otherwise dark drink.

> 2 ounces Canadian whiskey
> 1/4 ounce Fernet-Branca
> 1/4 ounce simple syrup
> 2 dashes Angostura bitters
> orange peel

Combine liquid ingredients in a mixing glass filled with cracked ice. Stir for 10 seconds and strain into a cocktail glass. Express orange peel over the glass, rub around the rim, and drop in.

Guggenheim Cocktail

The Pendennis Club, a social institution in Louisville, Kentucky, has played an important role in cocktail history. Not only was the Old Fashioned first mixed here, but in 1914, Jacques Straub, the club's head barman, authored *Drinks*, a book whose stated aim was "to satisfy the palate of the most critical connoisseur." Mr. Straub's legacy to the gentlemen of Louisville was the marriage of bone-dry vermouth with the rich aromatic sensations and crescendoing herbal bitterness of Fernet-Branca.

> 1 1/2 ounces French vermouth
> 2 dashes Fernet-Branca
> 1 dash orange bitters
> orange peel

Combine liquid ingredients in a mixing glass filled with cracked ice. Shake vigorously and strain into a cocktail glass. Express orange peel over the glass, rub around the rim, and drop in.

Old Hat

This long-ago "pick-me-up" was once en vogue with a loose affiliation of drinkers called the International Bar Flies, whose home base was Harry's New York Bar in Paris. In this riff on the original, Cointreau adds a cozy, orangey warmth to the bubbles of Prosecco, and Fernet-Branca crowns the drink with a layer of bitter, herbal savor.

> 1 1/2 ounces Cointreau
> Prosecco, chilled
> 1 teaspoon Fernet-Branca
> orange peel

Pour Cointreau into a flute glass. Top up with Prosecco. Hold a spoon directly over the drink, rounded side up, and gently pour Fernet-Branca over the spoon, creating a "float" on top of the drink. Express orange peel over the glass, rub around the rim, then discard.

Barbary Coast

The Barbary Coast was San Francisco's red-light district during the Gold Rush. Only desperation would cause somebody to mix Scotch and gin, but Prohibition was a desperate time. The origin of this cocktail is unknown, however this quote by Herbert Asbury sums up the rather shady character of this area of San Francisco as it was back in 1876. "The Barbary Coast is the haunt of the low and the vile of every kind. The petty thief, the house burglar, the tramp, the whoremonger, lewd women, cutthroats, murderers, all are found here."

> 3/4 ounce Scotch
> 3/4 ounce gin
> 3/4 ounce crème de cacao
> 3/4 ounce heavy cream

Combine ingredients in a mixing glass filled with cracked ice. Shake vigorously and strain into a coupe glass.

Dubonnet Cocktail

An international playboy with a striking resemblance to Fred Astaire, Paul Dubonnet inherited the drinks fortune built by his grandfather. The aromatic French aperitif earned its own eponymous cocktail, originally made from equal parts of the fortified wine and dry gin, topped off with a dash of orange bitters. Barmen fancied-up the presentation with a spiral length of lemon peel.

> **2 ounces gin**
> **1 1/2 ounces Red Dubonnet**
> **1 dash orange bitters**
> **lemon peel, cut into a finger-length strip**

Add gin, Dubonnet, and bitters to a mixing glass filled with cracked ice. Stir with bar spoon and strain into a cocktail glass. Express lemon peel over the glass and place on the rim.

Turf Club

A sibling of the Martinez was first concocted at New York's Turf Club, the gentlemen's club on the corner of Madison Avenue and 26th Street, where members gathered to play the horses. Albert Stevens Crockett immortalized this thirst quencher in *The Waldorf-Astoria Bar Book*, writing, "At times a good half – possibly two-thirds – of the crowd in the bar were interested in racing, and would appreciate a cocktail of such a name."

> 2 ounces Holland gin (Genever)
> 1 ounce Italian vermouth
> 1 dash Angostura bitters
> lemon peel

Combine liquid ingredients in a mixing glass filled with cracked ice. Stir briskly and strain into a coupe glass. Express lemon peel over the glass, rub around the rim, and drop in.

Princeton Cocktail

It was George Kappeler, head bartender at New York's Holland House Hotel, who attached the names of Ivy League institutions to a few of his original cocktails. Heavy and rich, port lends not only flavor to this drink, but when poured into the coupe glass with a steady hand, the wine settles on the bottom, creating a two-tone visual effect.

> 2 ounces Old Tom gin
> 2 dashes orange bitters
> 3/4 ounce ruby port, chilled
> lemon peel

Combine gin and bitters in a mixing glass filled with cracked ice. Stir briskly and strain into a chilled coupe glass. Gently pour the port into the glass, allowing it to slide down the side and settle on the bottom of the drink. Express lemon peel over the glass, rub around the rim, and discard.

Yale Cocktail

The 1906 Yale Bulldogs football team finished with a 9-0-1 record and was named national champion. That same year, students devised a cocktail using Blue Curacao to mimic the school color. Alumni embraced the drink which has endured many variations of the standard formula. This recipe is accepted as the standard.

> 1 1/2 ounces dry gin
> 1/2 ounce French vermouth
> 1 teaspoon blue curacao
> 1 dash orange bitters
> lemon peel

Combine liquid ingredients in a mixing glass filled with cracked ice. Stir briskly and strain into a coupe glass. Express lemon peel over the glass, rub around the rim, and drop in.

Skinner and Eddy

The road to the Dry Martini is paved with the odd and the eccentric. According to "Luscious" Lucius Beebe (moniker bestowed by Walter Winchell), Crosby Gaige was never known to shy away "when the ice in the shaker called stirringly to duty." His eccentric gin-based cocktail is named in honor of Ned Skinner and John Eddy, World War I shipbuilders, notable for breaking world production speed records for ship construction.

>**1 ounce gin**
>**3/4 ounce Yellow Chartreuse**
>**2 dashes orange bitters**

Combine ingredients in a mixing glass filled with cracked ice. Stir briskly and strain into a coupe glass.

Harry's Cocktail

Bartender Harry MacElhone acquired Harry's New York Bar in Paris in 1923. A year later, together with the journalist O.O. McEntyre, he organized a group called the International Bar Flies, an organization for serious drinkers with its own secret handshake and a necktie featuring a fly on a lump of sugar. Harry's became a magnet for Americans who traveled to Paris for drinks including a drink Harry named after himself.

> 2 ounces dry gin
> 1 ounce Italian vermouth
> 1 dash absinthe
> fresh mint sprig

Combine liquid ingredients in a mixing glass filled with cracked ice. Shake vigorously and strain into a coupe glass. Garnish with mint sprig.

Alaska Cocktail

"So far as can be ascertained," explains Harry Craddock in *The Savoy Cocktail Book* (1930), "this delectable potion is NOT the staple diet of the Esquimaux. It was probably first thought of in South Carolina – hence its name." In 1948's *The Fine Art of Mixing Drinks*, David Embury adds a measure of dry sherry to create an Alaska spinoff called the "Nome." Brrr!

> **1 1/2 ounces gin**
> **1/2 ounce Yellow Chartreuse**
> **1 dash orange bitters**
> **lemon peel**

Combine liquid ingredients in a mixing glass filled with cracked ice. Stir briskly and strain into a coupe glass. Express lemon peel over the glass, rub around the rim, and drop in.

The Bijou

Legendary barman Harry Johnson likely named this drink for colors of three jewels (bijous in French): gin for the diamond, vermouth the ruby, and Chartreuse the emerald – three components that come together agreeably for a refreshing and balanced cocktail. The original recipe called for equal parts gin, vermouth, and Chartreuse, but contemporary adaptations tame both vermouth and Chartreuse. (In Paris, the Ritz Bar version bid au revoir to Chartruese, partnering gin with orange curacao and dry vermouth). Its combination of gin, sweet vermouth, and Chartreuse is a classic mini-lesson in late nineteenth-century cocktailing.

> 2 ounces gin
> 1 ounce Green Chartreuse
> 1 ounce Italian vermouth
> 1 dash orange bitters
> lemon peel

Combine liquid ingredients in a mixing glass filled with cracked ice. Shake vigorously and strain into a coupe glass. Express lemon peel over the glass, rub around the rim, and drop in.

The Alberto

Dry, complex and aromatic, this drink appeared in W. J. Tarling's 1937 *Café Royal Cocktail Book*, its invention credited to A. J. Smith, a member in good standing of the United Kingdom Bartender's Guild. On the importance of mixology, Mr. Tarling writes, "In the morning the merchant, the lawyer, or the Methodist deacon takes his cocktail. Suppose it is not properly compounded? The whole day's proceedings go crooked because the man himself feels wrong from the effects of an unskillfully mixed drink."

- 1 1/4 ounces dry gin
- 1 1/4 ounces Lillet
- 1 ounce dry sherry
- 1 dash of Cointreau
- orange peel

Combine liquid ingredients in a mixing glass filled with cracked ice. Stir briskly and strain into a coupe glass. Express orange peel over the glass, rub around the rim, and drop in.

Atta Boy Cocktail

Almost every craft cocktail bar in London – and probably the world – has a well-thumbed copy of Harry Craddock's *The Savoy Cocktail Book* on the back bar, as this collection of more than 700 recipes remains, 83 years after its publication. Craddock exploits notes of pomegranate from the grenadine, adding complexity to his Martini archetype. Atta boy!

> 2 ounces dry gin
> 1 ounce French vermouth
> 1/3 ounce grenadine syrup
> orange peel

Combine ingredients in a mixing glass filled with cracked ice. Shake vigorously and strain into a coupe glass. Express orange peel over the glass, rub around the rim, and drop in.

Rolls-Royce

The drink first shows up in *The Savoy Cocktail Book*, the brainchild of Harry Craddock. Born in the UK, Craddock came of age behind the bar at New York's famed Knickerbocker and Hoffman House hotels, before becoming the best-known bartender at London's American Bar in the Savoy Hotel. Craddock likely created the Rolls-Royce cocktail, catering to the Bright Young Things of London society who congregated at the American Bar.

> 1/4 ounce Benedictine
> 1 1/2 ounces dry gin
> 3/4 ounce French vermouth
> 3/4 ounce Italian vermouth
> lemon peel

Fill a Martini glass with ice and let it sit until the glass is chilled. Once the glass is chilled, toss the ice, pour in Benedictine, swirl it around to fully coat the interior walls of the glass, then discard. Combine gin, and vermouths in a mixing glass filled with cracked ice. Stir briskly and strain into the prepared glass. Express lemon peel over the glass, rub around the rim, and drop in.

Tuxedo

Its name refers to Tuxedo Park, New York, at one time a refuge for Gilded Age high society and birthplace of the tailless suit, called, yes, the tuxedo. Before shuffling out of the city after work, Tuxedoites regularly stopped off at the city's top bars, most notable among them the Waldorf-Astoria bar, where this relative of the Martini was born. The drink was immortalized by Albert Stevens Crockett in 1931's *Old Waldorf Bar Days*.

> 2 ounces dry gin
> 1 ounce fino sherry
> 2 dashes orange bitters
> orange peel

Combine liquid ingredients in a mixing glass filled with cracked ice. Stir briskly and strain into a coupe glass. Express orange peel over the glass, rub around the rim, and drop in.

Alcazer

Prior to Prohibition, four compatriot barmen – Charles Christopher Mueller, Al Hoppe, A. V. Guzman, and James Cunningham – shook and stirred at 30 different bars around the country. Calling themselves "The Traveling Mixologists." Upon Repeal in 1934 they published a compilation of recipes titled *Pioneers of Mixing at Elite Bars*, intending to restore sophistication and good taste, along with reviving the lost art of their craft. In the Alcazer, they employ Cointreau to tame Fernet-Branca into a well-behaved glassmate. The onion donates an interesting salty-savory note on the finish.

1 ounce rye whiskey
1⁄2 ounce Fernet-Branca
1⁄2 ounce Cointreau
cocktail onion

Combine liquid ingredients in a mixing glass filled with cracked ice. Stir for 10 seconds and strain into a cocktail glass. Drop onion into the glass.

BOULEVARDIER

The drink first appeared in Harry McElhone's 1927 *Barflies and Cocktails*. It was created by Erskine Gwynne, expatriate writer, socialite and nephew of railroad tycoon Alfred Vanderbilt. Gwynne edited a monthly magazine, a sort of Parisian New Yorker, called *The Boulevardier*. Obviously, this is a Negroni with bourbon in lieu of gin.

> 1 ounce bourbon or rye whiskey
> 1 ounce Campari
> 1 ounce sweet vermouth
> orange peel

Combine liquid ingredients in a mixing glass filled with cracked ice. Stir briskly and strain into a coupe glass. Express orange peel over the glass, rub around the rim, and drop in.

Champs-Élysées

Known in France as La Plus Belle Avenue du Monde (the most beautiful avenue in the world), the Champs-Élysées is the Parisian center of commerce and culture as well as a source of national pride. A cocktail named for the famous street first appeared in Henry Craddock's 1930 *Savoy Cocktail Book*, although the original recipe doesn't specify Green or Yellow Chartreuse. This ambiguity allows some room to play, so use whichever you prefer.

> 1 1/2 ounces brandy
> 1/2 ounce Chartreuse (Green or Yellow)
> 1/4 ounce freshly-squeezed lemon juice
> 1/8 ounce simple syrup
> 2 dashes Angostura bitters

Combine ingredients in a mixing glass filled with cracked ice. Shake vigorously and strain into a coupe glass.

COPYRIGHT NOTICE

Nick and Nora: The Couple Who Taught America How to Drink is published and copyrighted © 2018 by History Company LLC (www.historycompany.com). All rights reserved. No part of this book may be reproduced in any form by any electronic or mechanical means (including photocopying, recording, or information storage or retrieval) without permission in writing from the publisher. Users are not permitted to mount any part of this book on the World Wide Web. Requests to the publisher for permission should be addressed to the Permissions Department, History Company LLC, support@historycompany.com

The publisher has made every effort to identify the rights holders in respect to the recipes and quotations featured in this book. If despite these efforts any attribution is absent or incorrect, upon notice the publisher will correct this error in subsequent reprints.

Limit of Liability/Disclaimer of Warranty: While the publisher and the author have used their best efforts in preparing this book, they make no representations or warranties with respect to the accuracy or completeness of the contents of this book. No warranty may be created or extended by sales representatives or written sales materials. Neither the publisher nor the author shall be liable for any loss of profit or any other commercial damages, including but not limited to special, incidental, consequential, or other damages resulting from the use of the information contained herein.

History Company books are available at special discounts for bulk purchases (shipping and handling charges apply). For more information, contact:

History Company LLC

www.historycompany.com

(800) 891-0466

Proudly Printed in the United States of America,

The Nick and Nora Glass

History Company offers a full spectrum of professional and custom barware, including Nick & Nora Martini Glasses for the most discerning bartender.

Shop the History Company Store on Amazon:
www.amazon.com/historycompany

Printed in Great Britain
by Amazon